Irish Cooking

Publications International, Ltd.

Favorite Brand Name Recipes at www.fbnr.com

Pictured on the front cover: Shepherd's Pie *(page 26)*.

Pictured on the back cover *(top to bottom):* Fish & Chips *(page 50),* Corned Beef and Cabbage with Parsley Dumplings *(page 36)* and Potato and Leek Soup *(page 12)*.

ISBN: 1-4127-2421-X

Manufactured in China.

8 7 6 5 4 3 2 1

Microwave Cooking: Microwave ovens vary in wattage. Use the cooking times as guidelines and check for doneness before adding more time.

Preparation/Cooking Times: Preparation times are based on the approximate amount of time required to assemble the recipe before cooking, baking, chilling or serving. These times include preparation steps such as measuring, chopping and mixing. The fact that some preparations and cooking can be done simultaneously is taken into account. Preparation of optional ingredients and serving suggestions is not included.

Contents

Whet Your Appetite

Beef and Parsnip Stew

1¼ pounds beef stew meat, cut into ¾-inch cubes
½ cup all-purpose flour
2 tablespoons vegetable oil
4½ cups canned beef broth
½ cup dry red wine
1 teaspoon salt
½ teaspoon dried Italian seasoning
⅛ teaspoon black pepper
8 ounces peeled baby carrots
2 parsnips, peeled and cut into ⅜-inch slices
¾ cup sugar snap peas

1. Toss beef in flour to coat. Heat oil in large saucepan over medium-high heat. Add beef and remaining flour; brown, stirring frequently.

2. Stir in beef broth, wine, salt, Italian seasoning and pepper. Bring to a boil over high heat. Reduce heat to medium-low; simmer, uncovered, 1 hour.

3. Add carrots. Cook 15 minutes. Add parsnips. Simmer 8 minutes or until vegetables and meat are tender.

4. Stir in peas. Cook and stir over medium heat until heated through.
Makes 5 servings

Patrick's Irish Lamb Soup

1 tablespoon olive oil
1 medium onion, coarsely chopped
1½ pounds fresh lean American lamb boneless shoulder, cut into
¾-inch cubes
1 bottle (12 ounces) beer *or* ¾ cup water
1 teaspoon seasoned pepper
2 cans (14½ ounces each) beef broth
1 package (about 1 ounce) brown gravy mix
3 cups cubed potatoes
2 cups thinly sliced carrots
2 cups shredded green cabbage
⅓ cup chopped fresh parsley (optional)

In 3-quart saucepan with cover, heat oil. Add onion and sauté until brown, stirring occasionally. Add lamb and sauté, stirring until browned. Stir in beer and pepper. Cover and simmer 30 minutes.

Mix in broth and gravy mix. Add potatoes and carrots; cover and simmer 15 to 20 minutes or until vegetables are tender. Stir in cabbage and cook just until cabbage turns bright green. Garnish with chopped parsley, if desired. *Makes 8 servings*

*Favorite recipe from **American Lamb Council***

Patrick's Irish Lamb Soup

Hearty Mushroom Barley Soup

Nonstick cooking spray
1 teaspoon extra-virgin olive oil
2 cups chopped yellow onions
1 cup thinly sliced carrots
2 cans (about 14 ounces each) fat-free reduced-sodium chicken broth
1 can (10¾ ounces) 98% fat-free cream of mushroom soup
12 ounces sliced mushrooms
½ cup quick-cooking barley, uncooked
1 teaspoon reduced-sodium Worcestershire sauce
½ teaspoon dried thyme leaves
¼ cup finely chopped green onions
¼ teaspoon salt
¼ teaspoon black pepper

1. Heat Dutch oven or large saucepan over medium-high heat until hot. Coat with cooking spray. Add oil and tilt pan to coat bottom. Add yellow onions; cook 8 minutes or just until onions begin to turn golden. Add carrots and cook 2 minutes.

2. Add chicken broth, cream of mushroom soup, mushrooms, barley, Worcestershire sauce and thyme; bring to a boil over high heat. Reduce heat to medium-low; cover and simmer 15 minutes, stirring occasionally. Stir in green onions, salt and pepper. Garnish as desired.

Makes 4 servings

Hearty Mushroom Barley Soup

Potato and Leek Soup

    4 cups chicken broth
    3 potatoes, peeled and diced
1½ cups chopped cabbage
    1 leek, diced
    1 onion, chopped
    2 carrots, diced
    ¼ cup chopped fresh parsley
    1 teaspoon salt
    ½ teaspoon caraway seeds
    ½ teaspoon black pepper
    1 bay leaf
    ½ cup sour cream
    1 pound bacon, cooked and crumbled

Slow Cooker Directions

Combine chicken broth, potatoes, cabbage, leek, onion, carrots and parsley in large bowl; pour mixture into slow cooker. Stir in salt, caraway seeds, pepper and bay leaf. Cover; cook on LOW 8 to 10 hours or on HIGH 4 to 5 hours. Remove and discard bay leaf. Combine some hot liquid from slow cooker with sour cream in small bowl. Add mixture to slow cooker; stir. Stir in bacon.   *Makes 6 to 8 servings*

Potato and Leek Soup

Irish Stew in Bread

1½ pounds lean, boned American lamb shoulder, cut into
    1-inch cubes
¼ cup all-purpose flour
2 tablespoons vegetable oil
2 cloves garlic, crushed
2 cups water
¼ cup Burgundy wine
5 medium carrots, chopped
3 medium potatoes, peeled and sliced
2 large onions, peeled and chopped
2 celery ribs, sliced
¾ teaspoon black pepper
1 beef bouillon cube, crushed
1 cup frozen peas
¼ pound fresh sliced mushrooms
    Round bread, unsliced*

Stew can be served individually or in one large loaf. Slice bread crosswise near top to form lid. Hollow larger piece, leaving 1-inch border. Fill "bowl" with hot stew; cover with "lid." Serve immediately.

Coat lamb with flour while heating oil over low heat in Dutch oven. Add lamb and garlic; cook and stir until brown. Add water, wine, carrots, potatoes, onions, celery, pepper and bouillon. Cover; simmer 30 to 35 minutes.

Add peas and mushrooms. Cover; simmer 10 minutes. Bring to a boil; correct seasonings, if necessary. Serve in bread.

Makes 6 to 8 servings

*Favorite recipe from **American Lamb Council***

Cheddar Potato Chowder

3 tablespoons margarine or butter
2 medium-size carrots, peeled and diced
2 medium-size ribs celery, thinly sliced
1 small onion, chopped
3 tablespoons all-purpose flour
¼ teaspoon dry mustard
¼ teaspoon paprika
¼ teaspoon ground pepper
2 cups milk
2 cups water
4 medium-size Idaho Potatoes (about 1¾ pounds), peeled and
    cut into ½-inch cubes
2 chicken-flavor bouillon cubes or envelopes
1½ cups shredded Cheddar cheese
4 slices bacon, cooked and crumbled (optional)
    Chopped chives (optional)

In 3-quart saucepan over medium heat, melt margarine. Add carrots, celery and onion; cook until tender, about 10 minutes, stirring occasionally. Stir in flour, dry mustard, paprika and pepper; cook 1 minute.

Gradually add milk, water, potatoes and bouillon. Bring to a boil over high heat; reduce heat to low. Cover and simmer 10 minutes or until potatoes are tender.

Remove saucepan from heat; add cheese and stir just until melted. Top each serving with crumbled bacon and chopped chives, if desired.
Makes 4 servings

Favorite recipe from **Idaho Potato Commission**

Carrot-Rice Soup

1 pound carrots, peeled and chopped
1 medium onion, chopped
1 tablespoon margarine
4 cups chicken broth, divided
¼ teaspoon dried tarragon leaves
¼ teaspoon ground white pepper
2¼ cups cooked rice
¼ cup light sour cream
    Snipped parsley or mint for garnish

Cook carrots and onion in margarine in large saucepan or Dutch oven over medium-high heat 2 to 3 minutes or until onion is tender. Add 2 cups broth, tarragon, and pepper. Reduce heat; simmer 10 minutes. Combine vegetables and broth in food processor or blender; process until smooth. Return to saucepan. Add remaining 2 cups broth and rice; thoroughly heat. Dollop sour cream on each serving of soup. Garnish with parsley.   *Makes 6 servings*

Favorite recipe from **USA Rice Federation**

Dublin Coddle

½ pound fresh Brussels sprouts
2 pounds potatoes, peeled and sliced ½ inch thick
1 pound Irish pork sausage,* sliced into 1-inch pieces
1 pound smoked ham, cut into cubes
½ pound fresh baby carrots
3 medium onions, cut into 1-inch pieces
1 teaspoon dried thyme leaves
½ teaspoon black pepper

*Irish pork sausage is similar to fresh garlic-flavored bratwurst. If unavailable, substitute
1 pound regular pork sausage and add 1 clove minced garlic with other ingredients in step 2.

1. Cut stem from each Brussels sprout and pull off outer bruised leaves.
Cut an "X" deep into stem end of each sprout with paring knife.

2. Place potatoes, sausage, ham, Brussels sprouts, carrots, onions,
thyme and pepper in Dutch oven. Add enough water to just barely
cover ingredients. Bring to a boil over high heat. Reduce heat to
medium. Cover and simmer 20 minutes. Uncover; continue cooking
15 minutes or until vegetables are tender. Remove from heat.

3. Cool slightly. Skim any fat from surface of liquid by lightly pulling
clean paper towel across surface, letting any fat absorb into paper. To
serve, spoon meat and vegetables into individual bowls along with
some of the broth. *Makes 8 to 10 servings*

Dublin Coddle

Pork and Cabbage Soup

½ pound pork loin, cut into ½-inch cubes
1 medium onion, chopped
2 strips bacon, finely chopped
2 cups canned beef broth
2 cups canned chicken broth
1 can (28 ounces) tomatoes, cut-up, drained
2 medium carrots, sliced
¾ teaspoon dried marjoram leaves, crushed
1 bay leaf
⅛ teaspoon black pepper
¼ medium cabbage, chopped
2 tablespoons chopped fresh parsley
Additional chopped fresh parsley

1. Cook and stir pork, onion and bacon in 5-quart Dutch oven over medium heat until meat loses its pink color and onion is slightly tender. Remove from heat. Drain fat.

2. Stir in beef and chicken broths. Stir in tomatoes. Add carrots, marjoram, bay leaf and pepper. Bring to a boil over high heat. Reduce heat to medium-low; simmer, uncovered, about 30 minutes. Discard bay leaf. Skim off fat.

3. Stir cabbage into soup. Bring to a boil over high heat. Reduce heat to medium-low; simmer, uncovered, about 15 minutes or until cabbage is tender.

4. Remove soup from heat; stir in 2 tablespoons parsley. Ladle into bowls. Garnish each serving with additional parsley.

Makes 6 servings

Pork and Cabbage Soup

Irish Meat Dishes

Irish Stout Chicken

2 tablespoons vegetable oil
1 medium onion, chopped
2 large cloves garlic, minced
1 whole chicken (3 to 4 pounds), cut into serving pieces
5 carrots, peeled and chopped
2 parsnips, peeled and chopped
1 teaspoon dried thyme leaves
¾ teaspoon salt
½ teaspoon black pepper
¾ cup stout, such as Guinness
½ pound fresh button mushrooms
¾ cup frozen peas

1. Heat oil in large skillet over medium heat until hot. Add onion and garlic; cook and stir 3 minutes or until tender. Remove with slotted spoon to small bowl.

2. Arrange chicken in single layer in skillet. Cook over medium-high heat 5 minutes per side or until lightly browned.

3. Add onion, garlic, carrots, parsnips, thyme, salt and pepper to skillet. Pour stout over chicken and vegetables. Bring to a boil over high heat. Reduce heat to low. Cover and simmer 35 minutes.

4. Add mushrooms and peas to skillet. Cover; cook 10 minutes.

5. Uncover skillet; increase heat to medium. Cook 10 minutes or until sauce is slightly reduced and chicken is no longer pink in center.

Makes 4 servings

Irish Stout Chicken

Pork and Cabbage Ragoût

1 tablespoon vegetable oil
1 pound pork tenderloin, cut into scant ½-inch slices
¼ teaspoon salt
⅛ teaspoon black pepper
1 cup chopped onion
4 cloves garlic, minced
1½ teaspoons crushed caraway seeds
8 cups thinly sliced cabbage (1 pound) or prepared coleslaw mix
1 cup dry white wine
1 teaspoon chicken bouillon crystals
2 medium Cortland or Jonathan apples, peeled and cut into wedges
Salt and black pepper
Instant potato flakes plus ingredients to prepare 4 (½-cup) servings mashed potatoes

1. Heat oil in large saucepan over medium heat until hot. Add pork; cook and stir about 2 minutes per side or until browned and barely pink in center. Sprinkle lightly with salt and pepper. Remove from saucepan and reserve. Add onion, garlic and caraway to saucepan; cook and stir 3 to 5 minutes or until onion is tender.

2. Add cabbage, wine and chicken bouillon to saucepan; bring to a boil. Reduce heat to low; simmer, covered, 5 minutes or until cabbage is wilted. Cook over medium heat, uncovered, 5 to 8 minutes or until excess liquid is gone.

3. Add apple wedges and reserved pork; cook, covered, 5 to 8 minutes or until apples are tender. Season to taste with salt and pepper. While ragoût is cooking, prepare potatoes according to package directions. Serve ragoût over potatoes. *Makes 4 servings*

Tip: For a special touch, stir ⅓ cup sour cream into ragoût at end of cooking time; cook over low heat 2 to 3 minutes or until hot.

Make-Ahead Time: up to 2 days before serving
Final Cook Time: 20 minutes

Pork and Cabbage Ragoût

Shepherd's Pie

1⅓ cups instant mashed potato buds
1⅔ cups milk
2 tablespoons margarine or butter
1 teaspoon salt, divided
1 pound ground beef
¼ teaspoon black pepper
1 jar (12 ounces) beef gravy
1 package (10 ounces) frozen mixed vegetables, thawed and drained
¾ cup grated Parmesan cheese

1. Preheat broiler. Prepare 4 servings of mashed potatoes according to package directions using milk, margarine and ½ teaspoon salt.

2. While mashed potatoes are cooking, brown meat in medium broilerproof skillet over medium-high heat, stirring to separate meat. Drain drippings. Sprinkle meat with remaining ½ teaspoon salt and pepper. Add gravy and vegetables; mix well. Cook over medium-low heat 5 minutes or until hot.

3. Spoon prepared potatoes around outside edge of skillet, leaving 3-inch circle in center. Sprinkle cheese evenly over potatoes. Broil 4 to 5 inches from heat source 3 minutes or until cheese is golden brown and meat mixture is bubbly.   *Makes 4 servings*

Prep and Cook Time: 28 minutes

Shepherd's Pie

Ale'd Pork and Sauerkraut

   1 jar (32 ounces) sauerkraut, undrained
1½ tablespoons sugar
   1 can (12 ounces) dark beer or ale
3½ pounds boneless pork shoulder or pork butt
  ½ teaspoon salt
  ¼ teaspoon garlic powder
  ¼ teaspoon black pepper
   Paprika to taste

Slow Cooker Directions

1. Place sauerkraut in slow cooker. Sprinkle sugar evenly over sauerkraut; pour beer over all. Place pork, fat side up, on top of sauerkraut mixture; sprinkle evenly with remaining ingredients. Cover; cook on HIGH 6 hours.

2. Remove pork to serving platter. Remove sauerkraut with slotted spoon; arrange around pork. Spoon about ½ to ¾ cup cooking liquid over sauerkraut, if desired.
Makes 6 to 8 servings

Ale'd Pork and Sauerkraut

Classic Cabbage Rolls

     6 cups water
    12 large cabbage leaves
     1 pound lean ground lamb
    ½ cup cooked rice
     1 teaspoon salt
    ¼ teaspoon dried oregano leaves
    ¼ teaspoon ground nutmeg
    ¼ teaspoon black pepper
    1½ cups tomato sauce

Slow Cooker Directions

Bring water to a boil in large saucepan. Turn off heat. Soak cabbage leaves in water 5 minutes; remove, drain and cool.

Combine lamb, rice, salt, oregano, nutmeg and pepper in large bowl; mix well. Place 2 tablespoonfuls mixture in center of each cabbage leaf; roll firmly. Place cabbage rolls in slow cooker, seam side down. Pour tomato sauce over cabbage rolls. Cover and cook on LOW 8 to 10 hours.

Makes 6 servings

Classic Cabbage Rolls

Pork Chops O'Brien

1 tablespoon vegetable oil
6 pork chops, ½ to ¾ inch thick
   Seasoned salt
1 can (10¾ ounces) condensed cream of celery soup
½ cup milk
½ cup sour cream
¼ teaspoon pepper
1 bag (24 ounces) frozen O'Brien or hash brown potatoes, thawed
1 cup (4 ounces) shredded Cheddar cheese, divided
1⅓ cups *French's*® French Fried Onions, divided

Preheat oven to 350°F. In large skillet, heat oil. Brown pork chops on both sides; drain. Sprinkle chops with seasoned salt; set aside. In large bowl, combine soup, milk, sour cream, pepper and ½ teaspoon seasoned salt. Stir in potatoes, ½ cup cheese and ⅔ *cup* French Fried Onions. Spoon mixture into 13×9-inch baking dish; arrange pork chops on top. Bake, covered, at 350°F for 35 to 40 minutes or until pork chops are done. Top chops with remaining ½ cup cheese and ⅔ *cup* onions; bake, uncovered, 5 minutes or until onions are golden brown.
Makes 6 servings

Microwave Directions: Omit oil. Prepare soup-potato mixture as above; spoon into 12×8-inch microwave-safe dish. Cook, covered, on HIGH 5 minutes. Stir well. Arrange unbrowned pork chops on top with meatiest parts toward edges of dish. Cook, covered, on MEDIUM (50-60%) 15 minutes. Turn chops over; sprinkle with seasoned salt. Stir potatoes and rotate dish. Cook, covered, on MEDIUM 12 to 15 minutes or until pork chops are done. Top chops with remaining cheese and ⅔ *cup* onions; cook, uncovered, on HIGH 1 minute or until cheese melts. Let stand 5 minutes.

Mussels Steamed in White Wine

¼ cup olive oil
1 onion, chopped
¼ cup chopped celery
2 cloves garlic, minced
1 bay leaf
½ teaspoon dried basil leaves, crushed
1 pound raw mussels, scrubbed
1 cup dry white wine
   Chopped fresh parsley, for garnish

Heat oil in large saucepan. Add onion, celery, garlic, bay leaf and basil. Add mussels and wine; stir well. Cover and steam 4 to 6 minutes or until mussels open. Discard any mussels that do not open. Garnish with chopped parsley; serve.   *Makes 2 servings*

Favorite recipe from **National Fisheries Institute**

Bacon and Cheese Rarebit

12 slices bacon
1 small loaf (8 ounces) egg bread or challah, cut into
   6 (1-inch-thick) slices
1½ tablespoons butter or margarine
½ cup beer (not dark)
2 teaspoons Worcestershire sauce
2 teaspoons Dijon mustard
⅛ teaspoon ground red pepper
2 cups (8 ounces) shredded yellow American cheese
1½ cups (6 ounces) shredded sharp Cheddar cheese
12 large slices ripe tomato

1. Cook bacon in large skillet over medium-high heat about 7 minutes or until crisp. Remove bacon to paper towels.

2. Toast bread slices until golden brown. Cover and keep warm.

3. Preheat broiler. Meanwhile, melt butter in double boiler set over simmering water. Stir in beer, Worcestershire, mustard and red pepper; heat through.

4. Add cheeses, stirring constantly about 1 minute or until cheeses are melted. Remove from heat; cover and keep warm.

5. Arrange toast on greased or foil-lined 15×10-inch jelly-roll pan. Top each serving with 2 tomato slices and 2 strips bacon. Spoon about ¼ cup cheese sauce evenly over each serving. Broil 4 to 5 inches from heat 2 to 3 minutes or until cheese begins to brown. Transfer to individual serving plates. Garnish with fresh herbs, if desired. Serve immediately. *Makes 6 servings*

Bacon and Cheese Rarebit

Corned Beef and Cabbage
with Parsley Dumplings

1 (4-pound) corned beef brisket, rinsed and trimmed
2 tablespoons TABASCO® brand Green Pepper Sauce
1 small green cabbage, coarsely shredded

Parsley Dumplings
2 cups flour
1 tablespoon baking powder
¼ teaspoon salt
1 cup milk
1 egg, beaten
2 tablespoons chopped fresh parsley
1 tablespoon butter or margarine, melted
2 teaspoons TABASCO® brand Green Pepper Sauce

Place corned beef in large saucepan with enough cold water to cover by 2 inches; add TABASCO® Green Pepper Sauce. Heat to boiling over high heat. Reduce heat to low; cover and simmer 2 hours, occasionally skimming surface.

During last 10 minutes of cooking corned beef, add cabbage to cooking liquid; return to boil over high heat. Reduce heat, cover and simmer 10 minutes or until cabbage is tender. Remove corned beef and cabbage to warm serving platter; keep warm. Reserve liquid in saucepan.

For Parsley Dumplings, combine flour, baking powder and salt in large bowl. Whisk milk, egg, parsley, butter and TABASCO® Green Pepper Sauce in small bowl until blended. Stir milk mixture into dry ingredients just until blended. Form dumplings by dropping tablespoonfuls of batter into reserved simmering liquid. Cover and simmer 10 minutes or until dumplings are cooked in center. Transfer dumplings to platter with corned beef and cabbage using slotted spoon.   *Makes 6 to 8 servings*

*Corned Beef and Cabbage
with Parsley Dumplings*

Lamb in Dill Sauce

2 large boiling potatoes, peeled and cut into 1-inch cubes
½ cup chopped onion
1½ teaspoons salt
½ teaspoon black pepper
½ teaspoon dried dill weed *or* 4 sprigs fresh dill
1 bay leaf
2 pounds lean lamb stew meat, cut into 1-inch cubes
1 cup plus 3 tablespoons water, divided
2 tablespoons all-purpose flour
1 teaspoon sugar
2 tablespoons lemon juice
Fresh dill (optional)

Slow Cooker Directions

Layer ingredients in slow cooker in the following order: potatoes, onion, salt, pepper, dill, bay leaf, lamb and 1 cup water. Cover and cook on LOW 6 to 8 hours.

Remove lamb and potatoes with slotted spoon; cover and keep warm. Remove and discard bay leaf. Turn heat to HIGH. Stir remaining 3 tablespoons water into flour in small bowl until smooth. Add half of cooking juices and sugar. Mix well and return to slow cooker. Cover and cook 15 minutes. Stir in lemon juice. Return lamb and potatoes to slow cooker. Cover and cook 10 minutes or until heated through. Garnish with fresh dill, if desired.

Makes 6 servings

Lamb in Dill Sauce

Stuffed Cabbage Rolls with Yogurt-Dill Sauce

1 large head green cabbage (about 3 pounds), cored
2 tablespoons olive oil
3 large green onions, sliced
2 large cloves garlic, minced
1 pound ground lamb
2 cups plain yogurt, divided
4 tablespoons fresh snipped dill, divided
1½ teaspoons TABASCO® brand Pepper Sauce
1½ teaspoons salt

Bring large pot of water to boil over high heat. Add cabbage, core end down. Reduce heat to medium. Cover and simmer until leaves are softened, 10 to 12 minutes. Remove cabbage to bowl of cold water. Separate 16 large leaves from head of cabbage. Trim tough ribs on back of leaves so that they will roll up easily. Chop enough remaining cabbage to make 3 cups.

Heat oil in 12-inch skillet over medium heat. Cook chopped cabbage, green onions and garlic until tender, about 10 minutes, stirring occasionally. Remove to bowl with slotted spoon. Cook ground lamb in drippings remaining in skillet over high heat until well browned on all sides, stirring frequently. Remove to bowl with cabbage mixture.

Process lamb mixture in food processor until finely ground. Toss lamb mixture with ½ cup yogurt, 2 tablespoons dill, TABASCO® Sauce and salt in large bowl; mix well. Place 3 tablespoons lamb mixture at bottom of cabbage leaf and roll up tightly to form 3-inch-long roll, tucking in ends. Repeat with remaining lamb mixture and cabbage leaves.

Preheat oven to 400°F. Place cabbage rolls on rack in roasting pan. Add 1 cup boiling water; cover pan tightly with foil. Bake 20 minutes or until rolls are hot.

Meanwhile, combine remaining 1½ cups yogurt and 2 tablespoons dill in medium bowl. To serve, remove cabbage rolls to platter; top with Yogurt-Dill Sauce. *Makes 4 servings*

Chicken Royale

4 boneless skinless chicken breast halves
1 package (4 ounces) Boursin or other herb-flavored cheese, quartered
½ cup English walnuts, finely chopped
4 large spinach leaves, steamed slightly
½ teaspoon salt
½ teaspoon black pepper
½ cup dry white wine
½ cup bottled reduced calorie raspberry vinaigrette dressing
1 tablespoon margarine
   Hot cooked rice

Pound chicken breasts to ¼-inch thickness with flat side of meat mallet or chef's knife. Roll cheese in walnuts. Place 1 spinach leaf on each chicken breast; top with a cheese quarter. Fold chicken around spinach and cheese to form a mound. Sprinkle salt and pepper over chicken. Place chicken in baking pan. Cover; bake in 350°F oven 30 minutes or until chicken is fork-tender.

Mix wine and dressing in small skillet. Cook over medium heat until sauce is reduced by half; stir in margarine. Pour sauce over chicken. Serve with rice.   *Makes 4 servings*

*Favorite recipe from **Delmarva Poultry Industry, Inc.***

Corned Beef Dinner

1 corned beef brisket (about 5 pounds)
2 medium onions, peeled and quartered
4 peppercorns
1 bay leaf
½ teaspoon rosemary, crushed
1 quart water
6 medium potatoes (about 2 pounds), peeled and quartered
6 medium carrots, peeled and cut into 2-inch pieces
1 cup celery, cut into 2-inch pieces
1 medium head green cabbage, cut into wedges

Horseradish Sauce
2 tablespoons CRISCO® Stick or 2 tablespoons CRISCO®
  all-vegetable shortening
2 tablespoons all-purpose flour
½ teaspoon salt
⅛ teaspoon black pepper
1 egg yolk
1 cup milk
2 teaspoons prepared horseradish, or to taste
1 tablespoon lemon juice

1. Place beef in large Dutch oven with tight-fitting cover. Add onions, peppercorns, bay leaf, rosemary and water. Bring to a boil; simmer covered for 3½ hours or until meat is fork tender.

2. Add potatoes, carrots and celery to Dutch oven. Place cabbage on top of meat. Cover and cook for 1 hour or until tender.

3. Meanwhile for Horseradish Sauce, melt shortening in saucepan over medium heat. Stir in flour, salt and pepper. Mix well and cook until bubbly, about 1 minute. Remove from heat. Beat egg yolk; add milk and mix well. Stir into shortening mixture. Cook over medium heat, stirring constantly for 3 minutes or until smooth and thickened. Remove from heat. Stir in horseradish and lemon juice.

4. Remove vegetables and meat to large platter. Serve with Horseradish Sauce.

Makes 12 servings

Totally Tuber

Roasted Potatoes and Pearl Onions

3 pounds red potatoes, well-scrubbed and cut into 1½-inch cubes
1 package (10 ounces) pearl onions, peeled
2 tablespoons olive oil
2 teaspoons dried basil leaves or thyme leaves
1 teaspoon paprika
¾ teaspoon salt
¾ teaspoon dried rosemary
¾ teaspoon black pepper

1. Preheat oven to 400°F. Spray large shallow roasting pan (do not use glass baking dish or potatoes will not brown) with nonstick cooking spray.

2. Add potatoes and onions to pan; drizzle with oil. Combine basil, paprika, salt, rosemary and pepper in small bowl; mix well. Sprinkle over potatoes and onions; toss well to coat lightly with oil and seasonings.

3. Bake 20 minutes; toss well. Continue baking 15 to 20 minutes or until potatoes are browned and tender. *Makes 8 servings*

Roasted Potatoes and Pearl Onions

Corned Beef Hash

2 large russet potatoes, peeled and cut into ½-inch cubes
½ teaspoon salt
¼ teaspoon black pepper
¼ cup butter or margarine
1 large onion, chopped
8 ounces corned beef, finely chopped
1 tablespoon prepared horseradish, drained
¼ cup whipping cream (optional)
4 poached or fried eggs

1. Place potatoes in 10-inch skillet. Cover potatoes with water. Bring to a boil over high heat. Reduce heat to low; simmer 6 minutes. (Potatoes will be firm.) Drain potatoes in colander; sprinkle with salt and pepper.

2. Wipe out skillet with paper towel. Add butter and onion; cook and stir over medium-high heat 5 minutes. Stir in corned beef, horseradish and potatoes; mix well. Press down mixture with spatula to flatten into compact layer.

3. Reduce heat to low. Drizzle cream evenly over mixture, if desired. Cook 10 to 15 minutes. Turn mixture with spatula; pat down and continue cooking 10 to 15 minutes or until bottom is well browned. Top each serving with poached egg. Serve immediately. Garnish, if desired.

Makes 4 servings

Warm Potato & Bean Salad

    16 small red new potatoes, halved
     1 large green or red bell pepper, cut into 1-inch squares
     3 tablespoons Italian dressing, divided
     1 can (15 ounces) kidney or pinto beans, rinsed and drained
     2 large green onions with tops, chopped
     1 teaspoon dried parsley flakes

1. Prepare barbecue grill for direct cooking.

2. Place potatoes in large saucepan; cover with water. Bring potatoes to a boil over high heat. Cook 9 minutes or until barely fork-tender. Drain; rinse under cold running water.

3. Alternately thread potatoes and bell pepper on 4 long metal skewers, or place on vegetable grilling grid. Brush 2 tablespoons dressing evenly over vegetables.

4. Place skewers on barbecue grid. Grill, on covered grill, over hot coals 10 minutes or until potatoes are tender, turning skewers halfway through grilling time.

5. Meanwhile, combine remaining 1 tablespoon dressing, beans, green onions and parsley in large serving bowl. Remove vegetables from skewers into bowl; toss well. Serve immediately.

Makes 4 servings

Serving Suggestion: Sliced tomatoes and green chili cornbread make a great accompaniment to this salad.

Tip: Use canned whole white potatoes, cut into halves. No need to parboil; just skewer with bell pepper squares.

Prep and Cook Time: 22 minutes

Fish & Chips

¾ cup all-purpose flour
½ cup flat beer or lemon-lime carbonated beverage
   Vegetable oil
4 medium russet potatoes, each cut into 8 wedges
   Salt
1 egg, separated
1 pound cod fillets
   Malt vinegar (optional)

1. Combine flour, beer and 2 teaspoons oil in small bowl. Cover; refrigerate 1 to 2 hours.

2. Pour 2 inches oil into heavy skillet. Heat over medium heat until fresh bread cube placed in oil browns in 45 seconds (about 365°F). Add enough potato wedges to fit. Do not crowd. Fry potato wedges 4 to 6 minutes or until outsides are brown, turning once. Drain on paper towels; sprinkle lightly with salt. Repeat with remaining potato wedges. (Allow temperature of oil to return to 365°F between batches.) Reserve oil to fry cod.

3. Stir egg yolk into reserved flour mixture. Beat egg white with electric mixer at medium-high speed in medium bowl until soft peaks form. Fold egg white into flour mixture; set aside.

4. Rinse fish; pat dry with paper towels. Cut fish into 8 pieces. Dip 4 fish pieces into batter; fry 4 to 6 minutes or until batter is crispy and brown and fish flakes easily when tested with fork, turning once. Drain on paper towels. Repeat with remaining fish pieces. (Allow temperature of oil to return to 365°F between batches.) Serve immediately with potato wedges. Sprinkle fish with vinegar, if desired.

Makes 4 servings

Irish Potato Soda Bread

1 medium **COLORADO** potato, peeled and coarsely chopped
½ cup water
¼ cup buttermilk
2 cups all-purpose flour
1 teaspoon baking powder
½ teaspoon baking soda
¼ teaspoon salt
¼ cup cold butter
2 eggs, beaten, divided
⅓ cup dried currants or raisins

In small saucepan cook potato and water, covered, over medium heat about 10 minutes or until tender. *Do not drain.* Mash until smooth or place mixture in blender; blend until smooth. Add buttermilk to measure 1 cup. In mixing bowl combine flour, baking powder, baking soda and salt. Cut in butter until mixture resembles coarse crumbs. Combine potato mixture, 1 beaten egg and currants; add to flour mixture. Stir until dough clings together. Stir mixture vigorously in bowl 12 to 15 strokes; form into ball. Turn ball of dough out onto lightly greased baking sheet. With sharp knife make a 4-inch cross, ¼ inch deep, on top of loaf. Brush with remaining beaten egg. Bake in 375°F oven about 35 minutes or until golden. Cool on wire rack.

Makes 16 servings

Favorite recipe from **Colorado Potato Administrative Committee**

Bubble & Squeak Casserole

½ cup condensed Cheddar cheese soup
¼ cup milk or chicken broth
2 medium red potatoes, cut into thin slices
2 sheets (18×12 inches) heavy-duty foil, lightly sprayed with
  nonstick cooking spray
1 small onion, cut into thin slices
2 cups shredded cabbage
¼ teaspoon salt
⅛ teaspoon black pepper

1. Preheat toaster oven or oven to 450°F.

2. Mix together soup and milk in small bowl until smooth. Set aside.

3. Place half of potato slices on each sheet of foil, overlapping slices. Top with onion and cabbage. Sprinkle with salt and pepper. Top with soup mixture.

4. Double fold sides and ends of foil to seal packets, leaving head space for heat circulation. Place packets onto toaster oven tray or baking sheet.

5. Bake 30 to 35 minutes or until vegetables are tender.

6. Carefully open one end of each packet to allow steam to escape. Open packets and transfer contents to serving plates.

Makes 2 servings

Serving Suggestion: If desired, top each serving with a fried egg or cooked sausage patty.

Bacon & Potato Frittata

2 cups frozen O'Brien-style potatoes with onions and peppers
3 tablespoons butter or margarine
5 eggs
½ cup canned real bacon pieces
¼ cup half-and-half or milk
⅛ teaspoon salt
⅛ teaspoon black pepper

1. Preheat broiler. Place potatoes in microwavable medium bowl; microwave at HIGH 1 minute.

2. Melt butter in large ovenproof skillet over medium-high heat. Swirl butter up side of pan to prevent eggs from sticking. Add potatoes; cook 3 minutes, stirring occasionally.

3. Beat eggs in medium bowl. Add bacon, half-and-half, salt and pepper; mix well.

4. Pour egg mixture into skillet; reduce heat to medium. Stir gently to incorporate potatoes. Cover and cook 6 minutes or until eggs are set at edges (top will still be wet). Transfer skillet to broiler. Broil 4 inches from heat about 1 to 2 minutes or until center is set and frittata is golden brown. Cut into wedges.   *Makes 4 servings*

Serving suggestion: Garnish frittata with red bell pepper strips, chopped chives and salsa.

Prep and Cook Time: 20 minutes

Cheesy Potato Pancakes

1½ quarts prepared instant mashed potatoes, cooked dry and
   cooled
1½ cups (6 ounces) shredded Wisconsin Colby or Muenster cheese
   4 eggs, lightly beaten
1½ cups all-purpose flour, divided
   ¾ cup chopped fresh parsley
   ⅓ cup chopped fresh chives
1½ teaspoons dried thyme, rosemary or sage leaves
   2 eggs, lightly beaten

1. In large bowl, combine potatoes, cheese, 4 beaten eggs, ¾ cup flour
and herbs; mix well. Cover and refrigerate at least 4 hours before
molding and preparing.

2. To prepare, form 18 (3-inch) patties. Dip in 2 beaten eggs and
dredge in remaining ¾ cup flour. Cook each patty in nonstick skillet
over medium heat 3 minutes per side or until crisp, golden brown
and heated through.   *Makes 4 to 6 servings*

Serving Suggestion: Serve warm with eggs or omelets, or serve
with sour cream and sliced pan-fried apples or applesauce.

Variation: Substitute Wisconsin Cheddar or Smoked Cheddar for
Colby or Muenster.

*Favorite recipe from **Wisconsin Milk Marketing Board***

Cheesy Potato Pancakes

Potato Rosemary Rolls

Dough
    1 cup plus 2 tablespoons water (70° to 80°F)
    2 tablespoons olive oil
    1 teaspoon salt
    3 cups bread flour
    ½ cup instant potato flakes or buds
    2 tablespoons nonfat dry milk powder
    1 tablespoon sugar
    1 teaspoon SPICE ISLANDS® Rosemary, crushed
  1½ teaspoons FLEISCHMANN'S® Bread Machine Yeast

Topping
    1 egg, lightly beaten
    Sesame or poppy seeds or additional dried rosemary, crushed

Measure all dough ingredients into bread machine pan in the order suggested by manufacturer, adding potato flakes with flour. Select dough/manual cycle. When cycle is complete, remove dough to floured surface. If necessary, knead in additional flour to make dough easy to handle.

Divide dough into 12 equal pieces. Roll each piece to 10-inch rope; coil each rope and tuck end under coil. Place rolls 2 inches apart on large greased baking sheet. Cover; let rise in warm, draft-free place until doubled in size, about 45 to 60 minutes. Brush tops with beaten egg; sprinkle with sesame seeds. Bake at 375°F for 15 to 20 minutes or until done. Remove from pan; cool on wire rack. *Makes 12 rolls*

Note: Dough can be prepared in 1½- and 2-pound bread machines.

Potato Rosemary Rolls

Totally Tuber

Scalloped Potatoes

    2 tablespoons margarine
    3 tablespoons all-purpose flour
2½ cups fat-free (skim) milk
    3 tablespoons grated Parmesan cheese
      Black pepper
    2 pounds baking potatoes, peeled and thinly sliced
      Ground nutmeg
      Salt
  ½ cup (2 ounces) shredded reduced-fat Swiss cheese, divided
    3 tablespoons thinly sliced chives, divided

1. Preheat oven to 350°F. Spray 2-quart glass casserole with nonstick cooking spray.

2. Melt margarine in medium saucepan; stir in flour and cook over medium-low heat 1 to 2 minutes, stirring constantly. Using wire whisk, gradually stir in milk; bring to a boil. Cook, whisking constantly, 1 to 2 minutes or until mixture thickens. Stir in Parmesan cheese; season to taste with pepper.

3. Layer ⅓ of potatoes in bottom of prepared casserole. Sprinkle potatoes with nutmeg, salt, ⅓ of Swiss cheese and 1 tablespoon chives. Spoon ⅓ of margarine mixture over chives. Repeat layers, ending with margarine mixture.

4. Bake 1 hour and 15 minutes or until potatoes are fork-tender. Cool slightly before serving. Garnish with additional fresh chives, if desired.

Makes 8 servings

Scalloped Potatoes

Round Out a Plate

Marinated Mushrooms, Carrots and Snow Peas

1 cup matchstick-size carrots
1 cup fresh snow peas or sugar snap peas
½ cup water
1 lemon
2 cups small mushrooms
⅔ cup white wine vinegar
2 tablespoons sugar
2 tablespoons chopped fresh parsley
2 tablespoons extra-light olive oil
1 tablespoon chopped fresh thyme
1 clove garlic, minced

1. Combine carrots and peas in 1-quart microwavable dish; add water. Cover; microwave at HIGH 4 minutes or just until water boils. Do not drain.

2. Remove several strips of peel from lemon with vegetable peeler. Chop peel to measure 1 teaspoon. Squeeze juice from lemon to measure 2 tablespoons. Combine peel, juice and remaining ingredients in small bowl. Pour over carrot mixture. Cover; refrigerate at least 3 hours.

3. To serve, remove vegetables from marinade with slotted spoon. Place in serving dish; discard marinade.   *Makes 12 servings*

*Marinated Mushrooms,
Carrots and Snow Peas*

Round Out a Plate

Roasted Fall Root Vegetables

½ pound potatoes
½ pound sweet potatoes
½ pound carrots
½ pound beets
1 cup chopped onions
3 to 4 cloves garlic, minced
4 tablespoons CRISCO® Pure Canola Oil
½ teaspoon dried thyme
    Salt and pepper to taste

Heat oven to 350°F.

Peel and cut potatoes, sweet potatoes, carrots, and beets into ½-inch cubes. Place them in large bowl; add remaining ingredients and salt and pepper to taste. Toss to mix well.

Place mixture on large baking sheet; bake for about 25 to 30 minutes or until vegetables can be easily pierced with fork.

Makes 4 to 6 servings

Note: Any variety of root vegetables such as turnips, parsnips, rutabagas, potatoes, carrots, sweet potatoes, yams or beets can be used in any combination. Use more or less as desired.

Roasted Fall Root Vegetables

Cabbage Wedges with Tangy Hot Dressing

1 slice bacon, cut crosswise into ¼-inch strips
2 teaspoons cornstarch
⅔ cup unsweetened apple juice
¼ cup cider or red wine vinegar
1 tablespoon brown sugar
½ teaspoon caraway seeds
1 green onion, thinly sliced
½ head red or green cabbage (about 1 pound), cut into 4 wedges

1. Cook bacon in large skillet over medium heat until crisp. Remove bacon with slotted spoon to paper towel; set aside. Meanwhile, dissolve cornstarch in apple juice in small bowl. Stir in vinegar, brown sugar and caraway seeds; set aside. Add onion to hot drippings. Cook and stir until onion is soft but not brown.

2. Place cabbage wedges, on flat side, in drippings mixture. Pour cornstarch mixture over cabbage wedges. Cook over medium heat 4 minutes. Carefully turn cabbage wedges over with spatula. Cook 6 minutes more or until cabbage is fork-tender and dressing is thickened.

3. Remove cabbage to cutting board with spatula; carefully cut core away with utility knife. Transfer to warm serving plates. Pour hot dressing over cabbage wedges. Sprinkle with reserved bacon pieces. Garnish as desired. Serve immediately.   *Makes 4 side-dish servings*

Cabbage Wedges with
Tangy Hot Dressing

Savory Matchstick Carrots

½ pound carrots, cut into julienne strips
1 small turnip, cut into julienne strips*
½ cup water
3 tablespoons butter or margarine, cut into chunks
1½ teaspoons fresh thyme leaves *or* ½ teaspoon dried thyme leaves
⅛ teaspoon *each* salt and black pepper
    Green onion tops and edible flowers, such as violets, for garnish

*Or, substitute two extra carrots for turnip.

1. Place carrot and turnip strips in medium saucepan. Add water;
cover. Bring to a boil over high heat; reduce heat to medium.
Simmer 5 to 8 minutes until crisp-tender.

2. Drain vegetables in colander. Melt butter over medium heat in
same saucepan; stir in thyme, salt and pepper. Add carrots; toss
gently to coat. Transfer carrot mixture to warm serving dish. Garnish,
if desired. Serve immediately.   *Makes 4 side-dish servings*

Savory Matchstick Carrots

Mashed Sweet Potatoes & Parsnips

2 large sweet potatoes (about 1¼ pounds), peeled and cut into
   1-inch pieces
2 medium parsnips (about ½ pound), peeled and cut into
   ½-inch slices
¼ cup evaporated skimmed milk
1½ tablespoons margarine or butter
½ teaspoon salt
⅛ teaspoon ground nutmeg
¼ cup chopped chives or green onion tops

1. Combine sweet potatoes and parsnips in large saucepan. Cover with cold water and bring to a boil over high heat. Reduce heat; simmer uncovered 15 minutes or until vegetables are tender.

2. Drain vegetables and return to pan. Add milk, margarine, salt and nutmeg. Mash potato mixture over low heat to desired consistency. Stir in chives.

Makes 6 servings

Mashed Sweet
Potatoes & Parsnips

Potato-Turnip Pudding

    3 pounds potatoes, peeled
    2 pounds turnips, peeled
    2 large onions, peeled
    ½ cup dry bread crumbs
    ½ cup FILIPPO BERIO® Olive Oil
    3 eggs, lightly beaten
    1 teaspoon white pepper
    ½ teaspoon salt
    ½ teaspoon ground sumac* or paprika

*Sumac can be found in Middle Eastern or specialty food shops.

Preheat oven to 350°F. Grease 13×9-inch pan with olive oil. Shred potatoes, turnips and onions in food processor using grater disk or by hand using metal grater. Discard any liquid that accumulates. (Grated potatoes will discolor quickly. If grating by hand, reserve grated potatoes in bowl of ice water to slow discoloration. Drain well before combining with other ingredients.) In large bowl, combine potatoes, turnips, onions, bread crumbs, olive oil, eggs, pepper, salt and sumac. Spoon into prepared dish. Bake 1 hour or until top is crusty and brown but center is still moist. *Makes 12 to 15 servings*

Honey Kissed Winter Vegetables

    2 to 2½ cups pared seeded ½-inch cubes winter squash
    1 turnip, pared and cut into ½-inch cubes
    2 carrots, pared and cut into ½-inch slices
    1 small onion, cut into quarters
    ¼ cup honey
    2 tablespoons butter or margarine, melted
    1 teaspoon grated orange peel
    ¼ teaspoon ground nutmeg

Steam squash, turnip, carrots and onion on rack over 1 inch of boiling water in large covered skillet about 5 minutes or until tender. Drain. Combine honey, butter, orange peel and nutmeg in small bowl. Drizzle over vegetables and toss to coat in heated serving dish.
Makes 4 to 6 servings

Favorite recipe from **National Honey Board**

Red Cabbage and Apples

   1 small head red cabbage, cored and thinly sliced
   3 medium apples, peeled and grated
   ¾ cup sugar
   ½ cup red wine vinegar
   1 teaspoon ground cloves
   1 cup crisp-cooked and crumbled bacon (optional)

Slow Cooker Directions
Combine cabbage, apples, sugar, red wine vinegar and cloves in slow cooker. Cover; cook on HIGH 6 hours, stirring after 3 hours. Sprinkle with bacon, if desired. *Makes 4 to 6 servings*

Mess 'o Greens

   6 cups water
 2½ pounds fresh smoked ham hocks
   6 bunches assorted greens (collard, chard, mustard, turnip, kale, spinach, etc.)
 1½ teaspoons LAWRY'S® Seasoned Salt
   1 teaspoon LAWRY'S® Seasoned Pepper
   ½ teaspoon LAWRY'S® Garlic Powder With Parsley
   2 tablespoons vegetable oil
   1 medium onion, chopped
    Hot pepper sauce, to taste

In large stockpot, place water and ham hocks; bring to a boil. Reduce heat to low and cook until ham hocks are tender, about 1 to 1½ hours. Remove ham hocks from water and remove meat from bone; discard bones. Finely chop meat; set aside. Clean and chop greens. Add greens and seasonings to water; bring to a boil on high heat. Reduce heat to low and cook until greens are very tender and have no bitter taste, about 1½ to 2 hours. Meanwhile, in medium skillet, heat oil and cook onion until soft and tender. Stir onion and chopped meat into greens. Serve with hot pepper sauce, if desired. *Makes 10 servings*

Meal Suggestion: Serve with cornbread.

Prep. Time: 18 to 22 minutes
Cook Time: 2½ hours to 3½ hours

Parsnip Patties

1 pound fresh parsnips, peeled and cut into ¾-inch chunks
4 tablespoons butter or margarine, divided
¼ cup chopped onion
¼ cup all-purpose flour
⅓ cup milk
2 teaspoons chopped fresh chives
 Salt and black pepper
¾ cup fresh bread crumbs
2 tablespoons vegetable oil

1. Pour 1 inch water into medium saucepan. Bring to a boil over high heat; add parsnip chunks. Cover; boil 10 minutes or until parsnips are fork-tender. Drain. Place in large bowl. Coarsely mash with fork; set aside.

2. Heat 2 tablespoons butter in small skillet over medium-high heat until melted and bubbly. Add onion; cook and stir until transparent. Stir in flour with wire whisk; heat until bubbly and lightly browned. Whisk in milk; heat until thickened. Stir flour mixture into mashed parsnips. Stir in chives and season with salt and pepper to taste.

3. Form parsnip mixture into four patties. Spread bread crumbs on plate. Dip patties in bread crumbs to coat all sides evenly. Press crumbs firmly into patties. Place on waxed paper; refrigerate 2 hours.

4. Heat remaining 2 tablespoons butter and oil in 12-inch skillet over medium-high heat until butter is melted and bubbly. Add patties; cook about 5 minutes on each side or until browned. Transfer to warm dish. Garnish as desired.   *Makes 4 side-dish servings*

Parsnip Patties

Maple-Glazed Carrots & Shallots

1 package (16 ounces) baby carrots
1 tablespoon margarine or butter
½ cup thinly sliced shallots
2 tablespoons reduced-fat maple-flavored pancake syrup
¼ teaspoon salt
⅛ teaspoon white pepper

1. Place carrots in medium saucepan. Add enough water to cover carrots. Simmer 8 to 10 minutes or until carrots are tender. Drain; set aside.

2. In same saucepan, melt margarine over medium-high heat. Add shallots; cook and stir 3 to 4 minutes or until shallots are tender and beginning to brown. Add drained carrots, syrup, salt and pepper. Cook and stir 1 to 2 minutes or until carrots are coated and heated through.

Makes 4 servings

Maple-Glazed
Carrots & Shallots

Tea Time & Beyond

Irish Flag Cookies

1½ cups all-purpose flour
1 teaspoon baking powder
½ teaspoon salt
¾ cup granulated sugar
¾ cup packed light brown sugar
½ cup (1 stick) butter, softened
2 eggs
2 teaspoons vanilla
1 package (12 ounces) semisweet chocolate chips
Prepared white frosting
Green and orange food coloring

1. Preheat oven to 350°F. Grease 13×9-inch baking pan. Combine flour, baking powder and salt in small bowl; set aside.

2. Beat granulated sugar, brown sugar and butter in large bowl with electric mixer at medium speed until light and fluffy. Beat in eggs and vanilla. Add flour mixture. Beat at low speed until well blended. Stir in chocolate chips. Spread batter evenly in prepared pan. Bake 25 to 30 minutes or until golden brown. Remove pan to wire rack; cool completely. Cut into 3¼×1½-inch bars.

3. Divide frosting among 3 small bowls. Tint 1 with green food coloring and 1 with orange food coloring. Leave remaining frosting white. Frost individual cookies as shown in photo.

Makes 2 dozen cookies

Irish Flag Cookies

Soda Bread

1½ cups whole wheat flour
1 cup all-purpose flour
½ cup rolled oats
¼ cup sugar
1½ teaspoons baking powder
½ teaspoon baking soda
¼ teaspoon ground cinnamon
⅓ cup raisins (optional)
¼ cup walnuts (optional)
1¼ cups low-fat buttermilk
1 tablespoon vegetable oil

Preheat oven to 375°F. Combine whole wheat flour, all-purpose flour, oats, sugar, baking powder, baking soda and cinnamon in large bowl. Stir in raisins and walnuts, if desired. Gradually stir in buttermilk and oil until dough forms. Knead in bowl for 30 seconds. Spray 8×4-inch loaf pan with nonstick cooking spray; place dough in pan. Bake 40 to 50 minutes or until wooden toothpick inserted into center comes out clean. *Makes 16 slices*

*Favorite recipe from **The Sugar Association, Inc.***

Shillelagh Sticks

8 slices bacon
16 garlic-flavored breadsticks (about 8 inches long)
¾ cup grated Parmesan cheese
2 tablespoons chopped fresh parsley (optional)

1. Cut bacon slices in half lengthwise. Wrap half slice of bacon diagonally around each breadstick. Combine Parmesan cheese and parsley, if desired, in shallow dish; set aside.

2. Place 4 breadsticks on double layer of paper towels in microwave oven. Microwave at HIGH 2 to 3 minutes or until bacon is cooked through. Immediately roll breadsticks in Parmesan mixture to coat. Repeat with remaining breadsticks.   *Makes 16 breadsticks*

St. Paddy's Pudding Pies

1 package (4-serving size) pistachio pudding and pie filling mix
   plus ingredients to prepare mix
1 package mini graham cracker pie crusts (6 crusts)
   Assorted candies and colored sprinkles
   Green gumdrops

1. Prepare pudding according to package directions. Divide pudding evenly among crusts. Decorate with candies and sprinkles as desired.

2. For gumdrop shamrocks, roll gumdrops on heavily sugared surface until fairly flat; cut into shamrock shapes with small cookie cutter. Place in centers of pies. Refrigerate leftovers.

Makes 6 servings

Honey Currant Scones

2½ cups all-purpose flour
  2 teaspoons grated orange peel
  1 teaspoon baking powder
  ½ teaspoon baking soda
  ½ teaspoon salt
  ½ cup cold butter or margarine
  ½ cup currants
  ½ cup sour cream
  ⅓ cup honey
  1 egg, slightly beaten

Preheat oven to 375°F. Grease baking sheet; set aside.

Combine flour, orange peel, baking powder, baking soda and salt in large bowl. Cut in butter with pastry blender or 2 knives until mixture resembles coarse crumbs. Add currants. Combine sour cream, honey and egg in medium bowl until well blended. Stir into flour mixture until soft dough forms. Turn out dough onto lightly floured surface. Knead dough 10 times. Shape dough into 8-inch square. Cut into 4 squares; cut each square diagonally in half, making 8 triangles. Place triangles 1 inch apart on prepared baking sheet.

Bake 15 to 20 minutes or until golden brown and wooden pick inserted in centers comes out clean. Remove from baking sheet. Cool on wire rack 10 minutes. Serve warm or cool completely.

Makes 8 scones

Favorite recipe from **National Honey Board**

Honey Currant Scones

Irish Chocolate Mint Dessert

1½ cups (3 sticks) plus 6 tablespoons butter or margarine, divided
2 cups granulated sugar
2 teaspoons vanilla extract
4 eggs
¾ cup HERSHEY'S Cocoa
1 cup all-purpose flour
½ teaspoon baking powder
2⅔ cups powdered sugar
1 tablespoon plus 1 teaspoon water
1 teaspoon mint extract
4 drops green food color
1 cup HERSHEY'S Semi-Sweet Chocolate Chips

1. Heat oven to 350°F. Grease 13×9×2-inch baking pan.

2. Place 1 cup (2 sticks) butter in large microwave-safe bowl; cover. Microwave at HIGH (100%) 2 minutes or until melted. Stir in granulated sugar and vanilla. Add eggs; beat well. Add cocoa, flour and baking powder; beat until well blended. Pour batter into prepared pan.

3. Bake 30 to 35 minutes or until wooden pick inserted in center comes out clean. Cool completely in pan on wire rack.

4. Prepare mint cream center by combining powdered sugar, ½ cup (1 stick) butter, water, mint extract and food color. Beat until smooth. Spread evenly on brownies. Cover; refrigerate until cold.

5. Prepare chocolate glaze by placing remaining 6 tablespoons butter and chocolate chips in small microwave-safe bowl. Microwave at HIGH (100%) 1 minute or until mixture is smooth when stirred. Cool slightly; pour over chilled dessert. Cover; refrigerate at least 1 hour before serving. Cover; refrigerate leftover dessert.

Makes 24 servings

Irish Chocolate Mint Dessert

Shamrock Ice Cream Sandwiches

Butter Cookie Dough (recipe follows)
Green food coloring
1 pint ice cream or frozen yogurt, any flavor

1. Prepare cookie dough; tint with food coloring. Wrap tightly in plastic wrap; refrigerate until firm, about 4 hours or overnight.

2. Preheat oven to 350°F.

3. Roll dough on lightly floured surface to ¼-inch thickness; cut using 3½- to 5-inch shamrock-shaped cookie cutter. Gather and reroll scraps to make 12 to 16 cutouts. Place on ungreased cookie sheets.

4. Bake 8 to 10 minutes or until cookies are lightly browned around edges. Remove cookies to wire racks; cool completely.

5. Remove ice cream from freezer; let stand at room temperature 10 minutes or until slightly softened. Spread 4 to 5 tablespoons ice cream onto flat sides of half the cookies. Place remaining cookies, flat sides down, on ice cream; press cookies together lightly.

6. Wrap each sandwich in aluminum foil or plastic wrap; freeze until firm, about 2 hours or overnight. *Makes 6 to 8 cookie sandwiches*

Note: Filled cookies store well up to 1 week in the freezer.

Butter Cookie Dough

¾ **cup (1½ sticks) butter, softened**
¼ **cup granulated sugar**
¼ **cup packed light brown sugar**
1 **egg yolk**
1¾ **cups all-purpose flour**
¾ **teaspoon baking powder**
⅛ **teaspoon salt**

1. Combine butter, granulated sugar, brown sugar and egg yolk in medium bowl; beat until well blended.

2. Add flour, baking powder and salt; beat until blended.

Shamrock Ice Cream
Sandwiches

The publisher would like to thank the companies and organizations listed below for the use of their recipes and photographs in this publication.

American Lamb Council

Colorado Potato Administrative Committee

Delmarva Poultry Industry, Inc.

Filippo Berio® Olive Oil

Fleischmann's® Yeast

Hershey Foods Corporation

Idaho Potato Commission

Lawry's® Foods

McIlhenny Company (TABASCO® brand Pepper Sauce)

National Fisheries Institute

National Honey Board

Reckitt Benckiser Inc.

The J.M. Smucker Company

The Sugar Association, Inc.

USA Rice

Wisconsin Milk Marketing Board

METRIC CONVERSION CHART

VOLUME MEASUREMENTS (dry)

1/8 teaspoon = 0.5 mL
1/4 teaspoon = 1 mL
1/2 teaspoon = 2 mL
3/4 teaspoon = 4 mL
1 teaspoon = 5 mL
1 tablespoon = 15 mL
2 tablespoons = 30 mL
1/4 cup = 60 mL
1/3 cup = 75 mL
1/2 cup = 125 mL
2/3 cup = 150 mL
3/4 cup = 175 mL
1 cup = 250 mL
2 cups = 1 pint = 500 mL
3 cups = 750 mL
4 cups = 1 quart = 1 L

VOLUME MEASUREMENTS (fluid)

1 fluid ounce (2 tablespoons) = 30 mL
4 fluid ounces (1/2 cup) = 125 mL
8 fluid ounces (1 cup) = 250 mL
12 fluid ounces (1 1/2 cups) = 375 mL
16 fluid ounces (2 cups) = 500 mL

WEIGHTS (mass)

1/2 ounce = 15 g
1 ounce = 30 g
3 ounces = 90 g
4 ounces = 120 g
8 ounces = 225 g
10 ounces = 285 g
12 ounces = 360 g
16 ounces = 1 pound = 450 g

DIMENSIONS

1/16 inch = 2 mm
1/8 inch = 3 mm
1/4 inch = 6 mm
1/2 inch = 1.5 cm
3/4 inch = 2 cm
1 inch = 2.5 cm

OVEN TEMPERATURES

250°F = 120°C
275°F = 140°C
300°F = 150°C
325°F = 160°C
350°F = 180°C
375°F = 190°C
400°F = 200°C
425°F = 220°C
450°F = 230°C

BAKING PAN SIZES

Utensil	Size in Inches/Quarts	Metric Volume	Size in Centimeters
Baking or Cake Pan (square or rectangular)	8×8×2	2 L	20×20×5
	9×9×2	2.5 L	23×23×5
	12×8×2	3 L	30×20×5
	13×9×2	3.5 L	33×23×5
Loaf Pan	8×4×3	1.5 L	20×10×7
	9×5×3	2 L	23×13×7
Round Layer Cake Pan	8×1½	1.2 L	20×4
	9×1½	1.5 L	23×4
Pie Plate	8×1¼	750 mL	20×3
	9×1¼	1 L	23×3
Baking Dish or Casserole	1 quart	1 L	—
	1½ quart	1.5 L	—
	2 quart	2 L	—